SIMPLY

COLOUR

50 CREATIVE IDEAS FOR IMPROVING YOUR HOME

LINDA BARKER

PHOTOGRAPHY BY LIZZIE ORME

ANAYA PUBLISHERS LTD
LONDON

For Jane, Jill, Sally and Ted

First published in Great Britain in 1994 by

Anaya Publishers Ltd
Strode House, 44-50 Osnaburgh Street, London NW1 3ND

Copyright © Anaya Publishers Ltd 1994

Editor	Emma Callery
Design	Watermark Communications Group Ltd
Photographer	Lizzie Orme
Assisted by	Adam Robinson
Stylist	Linda Barker
Jacket Design	Watermark Communications Group Ltd

With thanks to Ted and Vicky for the location

British Library Cataloguing in Publication Data
Barker, Linda
Simply Colour: 50 Creative Ideas
for Improving Your Home
1. Title 11. Orme, Lizzie
747.94

ISBN 1-85470-223-8
Typeset in Great Britain by
Watermark Communications Group Ltd
Colour reproduction by HBM Print Pte, Singapore
Printed and bound in Malaysia by Times Offset Ltd

Contents

Introduction

7

INTRODUCTION

Colour is available to everyone and it comes in many guises each of which can be quick to use. Paint and fabric are the most obvious materials, but don't forget the less conventional forms of colour - dyes and crayons, beads and sequins, even plastic - each is just as colourful. I have a unique rag rug created by a brilliant designer who uses plastic shopping bags hooked in with more conventional fabrics to create a stunning effect. In this book, I too have used shopping bags - this time for painting with. And why not? You will discover some wonderful results and here I show you how to do it simply, step by step. In fact, painting with shopping bags isn't as messy as you may at first think, best of all there's no need to wash out the brushes. It has to be my favourite way of painting walls at the moment. It's good fun and, as I will show you in this book, you can achieve some glorious finishes using strong or soft, delicate colours.

We can also learn a lot by watching children at play, young children in particular. They instinctively collect odd assortments of coloured ribbons and scraps of fabric along with pretty beads and shiny plastic. I envy my small nieces' collections of shells and pebbles; their pieces of flotsam and jetsam hang from the kitchen ceiling and these treasures often find their way into my photographic work as a stylist. In a way, I have borrowed their sense of wonderment and excitement from these innocent collections and used this approach in my own work. It is the memory of rummaging through my mother's sewing box, finding coloured threads and scraps of pretty fabrics, that led me to create the ribbon and organza placemats in this book. Their sequins and glitter thread glint so attractively, appealing to both the sophisticated and the innocent. Along with these materials you will see that I also like to make good use of broken china and the odd coloured tile

to produce delicate mosaics on walls or simply to decorate an otherwise featureless surface such as a flower trough. The humble junk shop and car boot sales were regular hunting grounds for many of the materials I use in this book. Not even the grubby cardboard boxes tucked under the sales' counter escaped my eagle eye and more often than not these revealed a magpie's nest of glittering bits and pieces.

It can be very refreshing to see odd assortments of glass and china that you thought would never go together somehow complementing each other brilliantly. Take a rusty old baking tray with some crystal candelabra drops and immediately a source of inspiration is found. Observe how a neglected brass candlestick starts to oxidize and turn green with verdigris; all of these are such fabulous colours, found quite naturally in everyday life. In this book I'll show you how to accelerate the natural verdigris process using special products that mean you don't have to wait ten years for Mother Nature to take its effect.

Accidentally stumbling upon materials that work brilliantly together can also work for colours. Quite often, colours of the same density vie for attention if they are put together and your eye becomes confused, darting between the two, making you feel uneasy. However, on a small scale, vibrant orange and lime green - such as those used on my gerbera bowl - produce an exciting explosion of colour. Rules are there to be broken, experiment with colour by painting on to scraps of paper and build up a small collage to see how different colours work together. Use the same approach for fabrics, beads and ribbons, assembling all kinds of bits and pieces; take some pieces out, add more of another colour. In this way you will develop a palette of colours that are particular to your own tastes and to no one else's. I've always loved orange curtains in my lilac room anyhow!

There are so many ordinary, everyday products and materials that can be used creatively, too. Take conventional powder filler, normally associated with boring jobs such as filling the holes in your walls or cracked skirting boards - you probably have an old packet at the back of your cupboard. Well don't throw it out because it takes on a whole new lease of life when mixed with emulsion paint. It produces the most wondrous gooey mess that can be piped, like icing, around a picture frame and it then dries rock hard. Or spread it over plastic flower vases, together with coils of string, to transform ugly pieces of utility plastic into *objets d'art*; well almost. Tin cans and dusty old biscuit tins don't escape the paintbrush either and if you thought the photocopier was for the office then think again. I bet you never imagined covering your walls with colour photocopies such as those featured here in the kitchen on page 64.

Above all else I want you to enjoy colouring your home be it in a small way by adding a coloured lampshade or a large way by colourwashing your walls, and I hope I can inspire you to be adventurous in your decoration.

Equipment

A magpie's collection of bits and pieces is all you really need to get going and a place to work - there's nothing quite as infuriating as having to clear away all your carefully arranged mosaic pieces ready for sticking just as you're getting going. A shed at the bottom of the garden would be fine if you can shut the door and be left alone to get on with it. Unfortunately, gardens are as expensive as houses in London, where I work, so that romantic concept unhappily doesn't apply to me. However, I have a wonderful studio with drawers full of shells and ribbons, vibrant squares of felt, paint, feathers, beads and coloured papers. Nevertheless, a table top is perfectly alright so long as you can spread your materials out in front of you.

Paint charts Invariably we have to rely on these tiny charts when choosing our wall colours, a very difficult thing to do. The trick is to take the paint chart into daylight if possible and preferably with a small swatch of the fabric that may be in the room. Hold the square at arms' length and squint at it to see the effect of the colour.

Paints I generally try to use water-based paints; not only are they kinder to the environment but they are simple to use and it is easy to wash your hands and brushes clean once the job is finished. Specialist paints such as ceramic and glass paints are available from good art supply shops or craft outlets. Always check the labels on these products to ensure that the piece of glass or china that is to be painted can be used afterwards or whether the painted objects are only for decoration. Gouache colour is an artist quality paint and it can be used thinly with lots of water to create a delicate wash or thickly to create a solid area of colour such as on the carrot image I used for the kitchen wall decoration.

Brushes For the painted projects you will need a selection of good brushes in several widths. You will need small brushes for craft projects and larger ones for some of the wall treatments - it is always good to pick up special offer multi-packs but be aware of the cheap and nasties. They may look alright inside the packaging but as soon as you start to paint they deposit stray hairs every second or third brush stroke, which becomes very irritating. When you've finished a particular project, wash brushes religiously. I always try to use water-based paints and use lots of warm soapy water at first and then rinse thoroughly, smoothing the hairs flat. Hang the bristles over the edge of a worktop to let the air flow around them so that they can dry thoroughly.

Art brushes are also available in many shapes and forms and although the initial investment may be high these should last a long time provided you care for them. I rarely use very fine brushes except for particularly detailed work. Hog hair brushes are perfect for the projects outlined in this book.

Inexpensive paste brushes are a good investment as they save your best brushes from ending up in the glue pot.

Varnishing requires a special flat brush available from art shops and good decorating shops and should only be used for varnishing, nothing else. I try to use water-based acrylic varnish whenever possible as the brushes can be quickly washed out in water.

Paint palettes and china saucers These are very convenient for mixing small quantities of paint or holding tiny amounts of glue and it is useful to have a stack of these to hand. Use your old ones, chipped ones or the hideous pink and purple ones that were part of a bargain gift set that your elderly aunt gave you for Christmas. Anything that saves the Royal Doulton.

Wax crayons Steal your children's colours to tint your homemade candles.

Sewing machines vary greatly, but the majority of the projects can be done using a straight stitch on any machine. A couple of projects use an embroidery stitch which your machine may or may not have. If it does, and you haven't used it before then I hope you will be tempted to do so as it is so simple to make the upholstery fringing which can cost a fortune in the shops. For those machines without this facility, I have always outlined an alternative that a basic machine will be able to cope with.

Pins and needles The fabric projects in this book range from small hand-stitched napkin rings, to more elaborate curtain treatments requiring a sewing machine of some kind, be it hand cranked or high tech. The enormous variety of pins and needles that are available amazes me, ranging as they do from semi-circular upholstery needles to the finest wedding dress pins. All that is required for these projects are the common dressmaker's pins and a packet of assorted household needles, available nationwide. I must confess, however, to being tempted into purchasing the odd wheel of pretty glass headed pins.

Fabrics The project that you are working on determines the type of fabric that is needed, and I always recommend a certain fabric for any one project. It is obviously sensible to use a washable fabric whenever you can, particularly on, say, a tablecloth or for some napkins. If more than one fabric is to be used for one project and you are buying the fabrics new, study the washing labels carefully, to ensure they are compatible for washing and that the colours are fast.

Fabric dyes These are sold in several forms: hot or cold water dyes, hand or machine dyes. I always try to dye fabric in a washing machine as it ensures an evenness of colour and is very convenient to use. Whichever dye you choose to work with, always read the manufacturer's instructions carefully first.

Bondaweb is a soft material that bonds fabric to fabric once it is pressed with a hot iron. This quality makes it ideal for appliqué and you will find it invaluable if you want to follow my instructions for the ribbon and organza placemats.

Ribbons and organza are materials that are always part of my basic work kit. These are generally bought as oddments or remnants and I am constantly adding to this supply: if I see a pretty ribbon, I may just buy it for my ever-growing collection, with the hope of it being just the thing for a future project. Car boot sales are excellent places for buying tied-up bundles of maybe six or seven different ribbons, of which several will be alright but one or even two will be particularly attractive.

Sequins, beads and buttons Buy these on a whim and store them in clean jam jars, on display if possible, to inspire new ideas.

Coloured papers and wrapping papers are lovely to have a supply of if you have the space to store them, and can then be purchased whenever you see one you particularly like the design of.

Filler and wallpaper paste Whether you are creating craft pieces of generally improving your home, general hardware supplies such as these are useful to have around. Once you discover my filler

and emulsion paint mixture, though, you may want to increase your supply.

Flotsam and jetsam What I would give to live near a beach! Shells and pebbles are all beautiful things to have to hand. At the moment I can't get enough driftwood or those glorious pieces of frosted glass that start life as broken bottles and the sea turns into little jewels. Feathers and bits of sheep's wool pulled from barbed wire on walks in the countryside, all these things are squirrelled away in my workshop awaiting transformation. Any other materials that are not mentioned should be familiar to most people but you will find an easy-to-follow ingredients list at the start of each project that you can quickly run through and check off before you begin.

CHAPTER 1

DECORATIVE COLOURS

The dining room was my starting point for many of the colourful designs in this chapter. The pine table didn't stand a chance, neither did anything else come to that matter - and my windows went through their third transformation this year!

Most of the projects in this chapter use elementary skills that most of us probably learnt as children. Also, practically everything can be made with very little money, a bit of effort, a bit of ingenuity and, for many of the designs, you may have the materials at home already.

Don't feel restricted to applying the techniques just to the surfaces I have suggested: the brightly coloured flower napkin rings are eye-catching on a small scale, but how about sewing seven or eight flowers on to a curtain tieback? Don't be afraid to experiment, and enjoy working with the colour in as many ways as you can think of.

Sunburst Sheer Drapes

Dying muslin is quick and easy in a washing machine and the choice of colours are infinitely more interesting than having to use either white or cream muslin. The sunburst panels can be attached quickly using eyelets.

MATERIALS

tape measure

cotton muslin

fabric dye

salt

sewing machine

thread

scissors

brown paper

pencil

canvas

self-adhesive felt

eyelets

hammer

ribbon

Hints

Enlarge the sunburst motif on this page on a photocopier to a 10cm/4in diameter. Then cut out the outline and use as a template. If you use ordinary felt, use a straight stitch on the sewing machine to sew the motif on to the panel.

1 Use the tape measure to calculate the amount of muslin you will need to cover your window. Allow 2.5cm/1in at the top and bottom for turnings and 7.5cm/3in at each edge for the zigzag detail. Add 30cm/12in to each drop for the sunburst panels. Dye according to the instructions.

2 Dry, then press the fabric and cut off the panel allowance. If more than one drop is used, stitch these pieces together. Turn over the seam allowances and stitch. Using overlapping corners of paper, create a zigzag template for the curtain edge and mark along the curtain edges using a pencil.

3 Stitch along the pencil zigzag line and then cut off the excess fabric using sharp scissors. Press, turning the excess fabric on the zigzags to the wrong side. To make this easier, you will need to snip the top off each zigzag point and snip into each zigzag bottom almost to the line of stitching.

4 For each width of fabric used, cut the extra piece of muslin into five 15 x 25cm/6 x 10in panels. Turn under the smallest seam allowance on all four sides to finish. Cut canvas panels 2.5cm/1in wider all around, fray three sides to a depth of 2.5cm/1in, turn under the top allowance and place the muslin panel on top. Cut the sun from the felt and glue in place.

5 Position the panels along the top edge of the curtain, spacing them out evenly so they have equal gaps between. Secure each panel on to the curtain with two eyelets using the hammer and simple assembly tool sold with the eyelets. Use ribbon to secure the curtain to the rail.

Leafy Table Top

Junk shops and car boot sales are great places for finding old tables or pieces of furniture that can be transformed with a touch of colour in this way. A lot of the hard preparation work can be done using an electric sander if you have one.

Hints

Masking fluid is very simple to use. It dries to a rubbery finish which can then be painted over and later peeled off. Wash the brush in warm soapy water regularly during the masking-off process to prevent a build-up of the fluid which otherwise would soon clog up your brush. The decorative detail looks best on the top of the table. Paint the table base plain, using green emulsion paint.

1 Prepare the table, stripping off any traces of old varnish or paint. Trace off our leaf on to thin cardboard and use the craft knife to cut carefully around the outline to get your stencil. Hold the stencil in place and use the old paintbrush to paint masking fluid through the stencil. Repeat across the table top, creating an informal pattern of tumbling leaves.

2 Use a household paintbrush to paint on the green emulsion paint; don't worry about trying to create a flawless finish as the surface of the table will later be distressed. Also, it doesn't matter if paint is brushed over the dried masking fluid as you can still see where the leaves are underneath.

3 When the emulsion layer is quite dry, peel off the masking fluid. You may need to start the process by rubbing the top of the surface with your finger which soon makes the rubber solution wrinkle. Sand the whole table using medium then fine grade sandpaper to distress the finish.

4 Use a fairly broad artist's paintbrush to paint boldly in thick strokes of pink acrylic paint on the leaves and dash in four quick strokes using the grey paint for the veined leaf detail. When this painting is quite dry, seal and protect the whole surface with a layer of antique wax.

Felt Notice Board

It seems to me that it is impossible to buy anything vaguely connected to the office in anything other than black, white or shades of grey. But most homes these days have a notice board of some description - even if it's only to pin the shopping list to - so customize your own with brightly coloured felt.

MATERIALS

notice board
coloured felt
scissors
PVA adhesive
glue brush
ribbon
ruler
decorative headed tacks
stapler (optional)
emulsion paint
paintbrush
masking tape or panel pins

Hints

Use a contrasting ribbon for the most dramatic effect or criss-cross lots of different coloured ribbons.

1 Carefully remove the frame from the notice board by stripping off the back tape or removing the fastenings. If these can be re-used, keep them on one side and use again when reassembling. Strip the old material covering from the board and glue down a piece of felt cut to the same size, using PVA adhesive.

2 Position the first piece of ribbon diagonally across the board and secure the ends with tacks. Use a ruler to position three parallel rows of ribbon on each side of this first one, keeping the distance between ribbons equal. Secure as before, then repeat across the other diagonal to form a diamond pattern.

3 Push tacks through the ribbons at the points where the ribbons cross. Remove the tacks from the outer edge and staple or glue these outer ribbons down. Use emulsion to paint the frame and wait for it to dry before reassembling. Secure the board to the frame using tape or panel pins.

CHAPTER 2

A SPLASH OF COLOUR

Brightly coloured kitchens get my vote every time and cooking in this Mediterranean-style environment inspires my creativity. If the carrots aren't quite to your taste, you'll find lots of other images in magazines or gardening publications that you could use as alternatives. How about a chicken, a flower or a topiary tree? Take your inspiration from books, designer showrooms and magazines .

As in Chapter 1, there is no need to spend a fortune on any of the projects here. You can recycle aluminium cans to provide the basis of decoration for the storage box and use it either to keep letters and trinkets inside or as a stylish tidy box for odds and ends. Make an ordinary little piece of furniture into a spectacular egg cupboard, or spice up a spice rack with a clever paint finish.

Kitchen Stool

These old-fashioned style stools can be purchased new or you might find them second-hand. They are usually brown or beige with natural cane or woven seats: nothing like the latticed checks that I have used here and, of course, the framework had to be painted bright blue to match.

MATERIALS

stool

2 colours of gingham

scissors

sewing machine

thread

staple gun

oil-based paint

paintbrush

Hints

Carpet tacks can be used instead of a staple gun to secure the woven strips, use two tacks at each end for extra security.

1 If possible, take the stool apart and remove all the old seat coverings from the seat base. Cut 7.5cm/3in-wide strips from the gingham, cutting each strip to a length that will cover the seat and provide enough allowance to be stapled underneath. Sew a small seam down the sides of each strip.

2 Cover across the seat base with horizontal strips of fabric. Pull each strip as tight as possible and secure with staples underneath the base so they cannot be seen. Don't worry about pattern matching as this adds to the final effect.

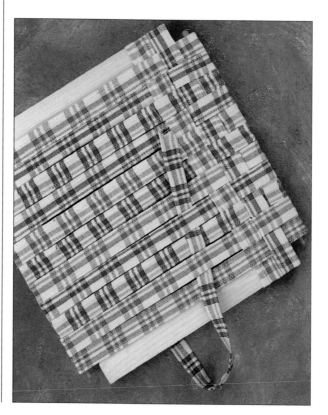

3 Thread the vertical strips through the horizontal bands, following a regular pattern of over one band then under the next. Alternate this procedure for each strip to create a tight lattice effect. Push each band close to its neighbour for a strong structure. Trim the strips underneath the base, paint the stool and reassemble.

String Vase

This wonderful vase started life as two plain plastic containers. I stuck them together and decorated them with a gooey mixture of paint and filler with the odd length of string thrown in.

MATERIALS

2 plastic containers

strong adhesive (epoxy resin)

filler

blue emulsion paint

old paintbrush

Hints

I think this spiral design looks good wrapped around the vase but you could shape the string into any number of different formations, or experiment with bands that are closer together or further apart.

1 Use a strong glue to secure the bases of the containers together and give them a good tug once they are dry to make sure they are going to stay stuck. Mix the filler with enough emulsion paint to give you a thick paste; you may need to add a little water as emulsion paints and fillers vary in consistency.

2 Cover the first 25cm/10in of string with some of the paste - be prepared to get completely messy at this stage. Lay the end of the string along the edge of one container and begin to bind it around the containers, painting on more paste as needed.

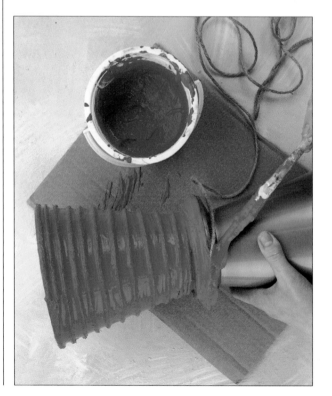

3 Continue spiralling the string around and take care to progress as neatly as possible over the point at which the containers join. The paste takes a little time to harden so there is time to remove the string and start again if necessary. Paint paste 2.5cm/1in inside the top rim and then leave to dry.

Egg Cupboard

The quality of this coloured photocopy is so good you would have to look twice to realize that it's not a high quality print. It's such a very clever way of turning a simple little cupboard into something out of the ordinary.

MATERIALS

glass-fronted cupboard	tin snips
chicken photograph	brown gummed tape
scissors	panel pins (optional)
hardboard	hammer (optional)
saw	oil-based paint or emulsion paint
chicken wire	paintbrush

Hints

Any simple glass-fronted cupboard can be given this treatment. The wooden shelves inside have been drilled at regular intervals using a 7.5cm/3in drill bit which provide just the right support for the eggs. It could also be used to display a collection of decorative eggs.

1 Select your favourite photograph of a chicken. If, like my photograph, the top of the print is dark, cut it away and replace with the lighter parts from another photograph to make a montage. Place it on a colour photocopier and enlarge it so that you have a print to fit the cupboard panel.

2 Cut the hardboard to the same size as the glass panel and glue the print on to the front. Snip out a piece of chicken wire using the hardboard as a template and lay it inside the glass door.

3 Place the hardboard over the chicken wire, ensuring the chicken is the right way up. Secure the panel to the door using gummed tape, and panel pins if necessary. If you need to use panel pins be careful not to break the glass: lay the cupboard on a padded surface and tap the pins in at an angle.

4 If, like this one, the cupboard has been varnished you will need to paint the frame using oil-based paint. If not, you will be able to use emulsion or water-based paints. Put in the wooden shelves and hang the cupboard securely on the wall.

Spice Rack

Distressed colour allows one colour to show through another and often works best when two contrasting colours are used together, as on this spice rack.

MATERIALS

plain spice rack

pink emulsion paint

blue emulsion paint

small paintbrushes

sandpaper (medium grade)

Hints

On larger objects you will find it easier to remove the top layer of emulsion paint from its base coat if you rub some hard wax between the layers.

1 Using pink emulsion and a small paintbrush to reach the corners, paint a base coat on to the spice rack. When this is dry, cover with a layer of the blue top coat. You needn't worry about applying this coat with the same careful coverage as for the first colour since most of it will be removed.

2 When the blue emulsion layer is quite dry, start to wear away the top surface with the sandpaper. It will be more interesting if you rub certain areas more than others and in some places the natural wood could even show through.

Appliqué Tablecloth

Use the boldest colours that you can find in your fabric department and don't necessarily be persuaded to use green for the leaves: I found blue and orange combine perfectly.

MATERIALS

scissors

fabric for leaves (blue)

chalk

Bondaweb

iron and ironing board

fabric for tablecloth (orange)

sewing machine

thread

Hints

Bondaweb makes appliqué incredibly simple as it secures the motif to the cloth and doesn't move until it is firmly stitched. If it isn't available you will have to resort to the labour-intensive method of pinning the leaf to the fabric with lots and lots of pins and hoping it doesn't shift as you machine or hand stitch it in place.

1 Use the enlargement facility on a photocopier to increase the leaves on this page to a size that fits your table. Be bold and go for dramatic, oversized leaves. Cut the leaf from the paper and use it as a template: position it on to the right side of the blue cloth and draw around its edge with chalk. Place a sheet of Bondaweb on to the wrong side, iron over it and then cut out the motif.

2 Place the blue fabric on top of the table to be covered and draw a freehand curve to represent the stem from which the leaves are falling. Cut this from the cloth, maintaining an even width of approximately 2.5cm/1in. Secure Bondaweb to the wrong side of the stalk. Iron the leaves and stalk on to the tablecloth fabric.

3 Use a close zigzag stitch on the machine to sew around the leaves and the stalk. Feed the fabric slowly under the sewing foot as the bends and twists on the leaves are tricky to negotiate at speed. If your sewing machine has one, finish the hem around the cloth with a decorative embroidery stitch, or use a zigzag.

Sunflower Plant Pots

The humble terracotta plant pot comes out of the garden shed.

MATERIALS

plant pots

white emulsion paint

paintbrush

blue emulsion paint

plastic container

cotton cloth

wrapping paper

scissors

PVA adhesive

glue brush

acrylic varnish

Hints

Any flowery wrapping paper or pictures cut from magazines or seed catalogues could be used to decorate these pots.

1 Paint the outside of each flower pot with a layer of white emulsion paint. Mix one part blue emulsion paint with one part water in the plastic container to make a diluted solution. When the white emulsion is dry paint this solution over the pot.

2 While the paint is still wet, remove some of the blue paint from the surface of the pot with a damp cotton cloth to reveal some of the white paint underneath. Keep turning the cloth over as the paint builds up and rinse it out occasionally.

3 Cut flower motifs from the wrapping paper. These sunflowers are quite intricate, but it is worthwhile spending time cutting away all the background colour. Glue the flowers on the flat surface of the pot and allow to dry before painting with acrylic varnish for protection.

Painted Tinware

These attractive tins started life as ordinary biscuit tins that are usually thrown out with the rubbish once the contents have been eaten.

MATERIALS

old tin

car spray paint

star template

masking tape

small piece of wood

hammer

nail

enamel paint

paintbrush

Hints

Always slide a piece of wood underneath the area to be punched and support it on a solid surface such as a table or workbench. Otherwise you'll find the whole panel will be punched in.

1 Remove any labels from the tin and wash with warm soapy water. Spray the outer surfaces of the tin with car spray paint. You will find this easier if you protect the surrounding area with newspaper as the spray paint particles get everywhere. Leave the tin for 10 minutes to dry thoroughly.

2 Enlarge the template on this page using a photocopier until you have a size that fits your tin, or draw your own heart or flower shapes. Fix the template over the area to be punched using masking tape and slide a piece of wood underneath. Make indentations by hammering the nail along the outline.

3 Peel the template from the tin to reveal the punched pattern underneath. You can then either leave the tin as it is or pick out details in the pattern using enamel paint. At the back of the punched panel you will notice the tin is quite sharp: tap the hammer over the points gently to knock these back slightly.

Mosaic Planter

Add a splash of colour to your windowsill inside or out.

MATERIALS

wooden planter	paintbrush
pencil	cloth
chisel	tile adhesive/grout
hammer	coloured tile
emulsion paint	strip of cardboard

Hints

Always work away from you when using cutting tools; it is all too easy to slip.

1 Transfer the simple line drawing from this page on to your planter using a pencil. Depending on the size of the planter, you may need to scale this drawing up using a photocopier, or draw your own motif directly on to the planter using this leaf as a guide.

2 Chisel along the outlines of the design using short sharp taps of the hammer to a depth of approximately 6mm/$^1/_4$ in. Then gouge out the wood inside the outlines using a specialist tool or the chisel. Try to maintain an even depth to the design.

3 Mix an equal quantity of emulsion paint with water and use this to paint the outside of the planter. While the paint is still wet remove some of it with a damp cloth so that the wood grain can still be seen through the painted surface.

4 Smash up the coloured tile between sheets of newspaper (see page 32). Then use the strip of cardboard to push tile adhesive/grout into the groove and press small pieces of the tile into it and allow to dry. Spread a further layer of adhesive/grout over the mosaic, wipe the surface with the damp cloth and leave to dry.

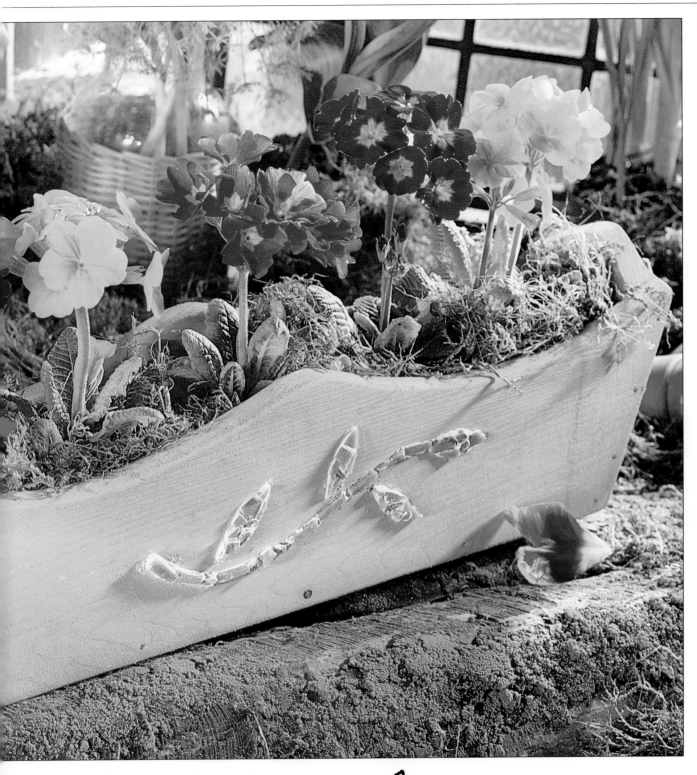

Roller Blind

Most plain bamboo roller blinds can be given this colourful treatment - match the colour to your walls.

MATERIALS

roller blind

emulsion paint

plastic container

paintbrush

fabric

scissors

PVA adhesive

glue brush

needle

thread

Hints

Stretch the blind gently as you paint it to open up the weave so these gaps don't become clogged with paint.

1 Mix together a solution of paint and water using equal quantities of each in the plastic container. Unroll the blind on to sheets of newspaper and pull back the cord to protect it from the splashy paint. Paint the front, leave to dry, and then turn over to paint the back.

2 Cut two strips of fabric to the length of the blind and one strip to the width of the blind. Each strip should be 7.5cm/3in wide. Stitch a small seam down the edges of each strip. Spread glue along the inside of the longer strips, fold in half and cover each edge of the blind with one strip.

3 Spread glue along the inside edge of the smaller strip and fold the ends inwards to make an arrow-shaped point. Fold in half and slip the blind inside the fabric strip as before. The arrow head mitres the fabric, making a neater finish.

4 Use an invisible stitch to secure the fabric binding to the blind. Push the needle through all the thicknesses, pull the thread tight and then pull the needle through to the front again. Continue along all three sides. Reassemble the cords and hang the blind according to the instructions.

Mosaic and Shell Border

Equally at home in the kitchen or the bathroom, this border makes use of broken china and tiles.

MATERIALS

scallop shells	tile adhesive/grout
pencil	broken tiles
Blue-tac	broken china
tape measure	cloth
thin cardboard	spreader

Hints

Using a damp cloth, rub the top layer of adhesive/grout from the surface of the mosaic before it is dry. Otherwise it could take you longer to remove this than it takes to build up the whole border.

1 To make the wave stencil, position the shells along the top of the wall tiles and mark their position with a pencil. Hold them in place with Blue-tac, measure the distance between the shells and transfer on to cardboard. Draw a wave between these measurements and cut out the shape.

2 Remove the shells from the wall and position the wave stencil between the pencil marks. Spread adhesive/grout through the wave stencil maintaining an even thickness. Prepare only two or three waves at a time or the adhesive/grout will have dried before the mosaic pieces are in place.

3 While the adhesive/grout is still wet, push the pieces of broken tiles and china into the surface, building up an intricate mosaic pattern. Move on to the next group of waves as one group is finished. When dry, spread more adhesive/grout on to the tiles, wiping off the excess with a damp cloth.

Harlequin Cupboard

We often cover the surface of shelves, but what about the back of a shelf unit? I think a simple treatment like this looks eye-catching both on open shelves or inside a cupboard.

MATERIALS

tape measure

pencil

ruler

coloured papers

scissors

wallpaper paste

paintbrush

Hints

Don't feel restricted to plain colours for this treatment: two designs of floral wrapping papers would have a pretty patchwork effect. I have used three diamonds along the length of the cupboard, but depending on the length of your shelves you may want fewer or more to cover the space.

1 To establish the width of the harlequin diamond, measure the length of the area to be covered and divide into three. To determine the height of the diamond, measure the distance between the two shelves. Transfer these measurements to the papers and cut out your diamonds in both colours of paper.

2 Glue the diamonds in place using wallpaper paste. Glue the whole diamonds first, then cut the others into halves and quarters to fill in the gaps. Repeat this procedure for each space until all your shelf back has been covered.

Two-toned Napkins

Use this panelling technique to make a small square of fabric into a large napkin: the more expensive the fabric, the deeper the border should be.

MATERIALS

plain fabric
patterned fabric
iron and ironing board
bias binding
sewing machine
threads (2 colours)

Hints

Choose fabrics that can be washed together and avoid those that are for dry cleaning only.

1 Cut the plain fabric to the required size of your napkin (40cm/16in is a generous size), but it could be larger or smaller as you wish. Trim your patterned fabric into a smaller square and turn under the raw edges with a hot iron. Choose a coloured bias binding to complement the fabrics.

2 Pin the patterned square on to the plain fabric ensuring the borders are even all round. Use a close zigzag machine stitch to sew in place. Stitch the raw edge of the binding to the wrong side of the napkin, turn over to trap the raw edge and sew closed. Use four separate binding pieces for the neatest edging.

Kitchen Wall Treatment

Colour each photocopy individually or use a colour photocopier, either way your kitchen walls will be far from boring.

MATERIALS

black-and-white photocopies

scissors

gouache colours

wallpaper paste

paintbrush

Hints

If you can find a vegetable print in a gardening magazine or catalogue, use this if you prefer.

1 Photocopy six individual motifs from the original on this page, enlarging if necessary. Then assemble these and place onto the photocopier so that the next copy has six motifs printed on it. Colour the motifs simply using two gouache colours, then copy this on a colour photocopier until you have enough motifs to cover the walls.

2 Cut each motif from the copy paper and paste these on to the wall using wallpaper paste. Arrange the motifs around the kitchen fittings as you wish: it is better if they don't form a regular pattern.

CHAPTER 3

COLOUR CREATIONS

Take inspiration from these terracotta walls and use the plastic bag style of painting to transform your home, using colours to suit your own taste. I've created a strongly coloured finish, but the technique works just as well using softer colours.

If you like the stencilled wall decorations in plaster relief - but not all over the wall - then use one motif spaced regularly at dado height. Be guided by the projects, but find your own solutions for your own home.

If you are planning something on a smaller scale, take the silk flowers out of the vase and sew them into a cushion or a tieback, it's often the surprise of the unfamiliar that catches your eye. Even the more conventional painted glassware is given an exotic touch with the addition of a few glass beads. Nothing could be simpler but the result is stunning.

Covered Footstool

Most footstools are covered in rather boring fabric and although I am using two colours of plain cotton, this method of cutting away one fabric to reveal another underneath is very attractive.

MATERIALS

scissors

2 pieces of contrasting fabric

chalk

pins

sewing machine

thread

staple gun

tacks

hammer

hessian

Hints

If possible, remove the legs from the footstool first as this makes fitting the fabric easier.

1 Cut the fabrics to fit over, around and just beneath the footstool. Baste the pieces together. Enlarge the template below on a photocopier to a suitable size. Use it to draw the stars on the top fabric, avoiding the fabric edges. Pin around the stars.

2 Use a contrasting thread and a close zigzag stitch on the sewing machine to stitch around the star outlines. Carefully cut inside the sewn areas on the top layer only.

3 Place the fabric right side down and lay the footstool over this. Pull the fabric over the sides and staple it to the underside of the stool, keeping the fabric taught.

4 Fold the corners to make neat mitred folds. Using tacks, attach a piece of hessian to the underside of the footstool covering the row of staples. Paint the legs to match the top and reassemble.

Sunflower Tiebacks

You could stitch any silk flower on to a tieback, but these sunflowers really brighten up a room.

MATERIALS

old tieback

hessian or plain fabric

sewing machine

thread

silk flowers

needle

tieback rings

Hints

Re-cover your old tiebacks using hessian or a plain fabric, or stitch the flowers on plain, ready-made tiebacks.

1 Using the old tieback as a guide, cut the hessian adding 2.5cm/1in all round for turning. Turn the allowance over on to the wrong side, press and then machine stitch in place.

2 Pull the leaves and flowers from their plastic stalks and stitch the leaves in place first, using long stitches. Then stitch on the sunflower head with as many stitches as it needs: it will look untidy at the back.

3 Cut another piece of hessian as before and press the allowance under. Sew this by hand on the wrong side of the tieback to hide all the stitching. Sew two rings on either end of the tieback to complete.

Coloured Woodstained Table

Coloured woodstains can be found in many colours in addition to brown mahogany or chestnut, and it is a refreshing change to see them used in this way.

MATERIALS

coffee table

tape measure

masking tape

craft knife

ruler

3 coloured woodstains

saucers

paintbrushes

furniture wax

Hints

Woodstain must always be applied to unfinished wood for the pigment to be absorbed. If you are using an old table, make sure it has been well sanded or stripped before starting. If you have a rectangular table, you may wish to have one long, thin diamond or three smaller ones in the centre.

Plaster Wall Decoration

Mix together coloured emulsion paint with ordinary filler and use a spreader to push the mixture through a simply-cut stencil for a unique wall decoration.

MATERIALS

manila paper

craft knife

pencil

filler

coloured emulsion paint

plastic container

spreader

double-sided tape

Hints

You could use thin cardboard for your stencil rather than manila paper, but paint it with two layers of oil-based paint first so that it doesn't go soggy.

1 Enlarge the templates from this page to an appropriate size. Trace the designs on to the manila paper and use the craft knife to cut out the shapes carefully. You will need to leave a border of at least 7.5cm/3in around the stencil.

2 Mix together enough emulsion paint and filler to make a thick but spreadable paste. If necessary, add a little water although I tend to find that most emulsion paints contain enough water. Mix thoroughly with the spreader to remove any lumps.

Living Room Wall Treatment

Strange as it may seem, this paint finish has been achieved using a plastic bag rather than a paintbrush. Thin washes of colour have been layered on top until the desired effect is reached.

MATERIALS

yellow emulsion paint

terracotta emulsion paint (2 shades)

paintbrushes

plastic bags

plastic container

mixing brush

Hints

This is a paint finish that definitely improves as more and more layers are added so don't be discouraged at the start - I warn you, the surface does look a bit messy!

1 Prepare the surfaces to be painted, then cover the floor and furniture. Start by applying wide splodges of both colours with a large paintbrush. I have used one shade of yellow and two of terracotta for this paint treatment. Work one area at a time, say one whole wall, then move around the room.

2 While the paint is still wet, press a crumpled plastic bag on to the wet surface and then lift if off and press into another area of wet paint. Continue all over the wet paint area, then repeat the process. You will need to replace each bag as it becomes saturated with paint.

3 Use pieces of double-sided tape to temporarily fix the stencil on the wall. Using the spreader, scrape the filler over the surface of the stencil. Don't overload the spreader or you may find the filler moving behind the stencil and spoiling the motif. Peel back the stencil and leave to dry.

3 Dilute one shade of terracotta with an equal quantity of water in a plastic container and mix together to produce a thin solution of paint. Apply this using a large brush to the surface of the 'bagged' paint using broad loose strokes as if you were cleaning the wall. Build some areas up using three or four washes like this and leave others with only one wash.

CHAPTER 4

COLOUR BY DESIGN

I f, like me, you're always keeping one eye out for ideas, and the other one on the decorating budget, then you can't go wrong with many of the ideas in this chapter. My stylish curtain banner makes economical use of expensive fabrics yet produces a stunning window display. The largest amount of fabric you will need for any one curtain is half the drop as you simply cut the fabric in half lengthways and then sew the two halves together, end to end. Follow my instructions for the curtain trimming to edge the banner, then dye muslin for the backing and sew together. It couldn't be easier and not only do you have a stunning look for your windows, it literally halves your fabric costs. Try my colour transformations on hat boxes, mirror frames, chairs and stencilled walls and you could even find yourself piping coloured filler on to your picture frames!

Stencilled Floorcloth

I love these simple, hard-wearing cloths because you can decorate them in whatever pattern or style you fancy. Let the children decorate their own bedroom cloth, covering the floor with lots of newspaper first. All you need to do is let the paint dry, then protect it with acrylic varnish.

MATERIALS

canvas

scissors

sewing machine

thread

cloth

iron and ironing board

pencil

ruler

emulsion paints

paintbrush

manila paper

craft knife

double-sided tape

stencil brush

Hints

For a completely no-sew project, you can glue the hems down using PVA adhesive.

1 Cut the canvas to the size of cloth you require plus 5cm/2in all around for the hem. Turn the hem under, machine stitch and then press down firmly with a damp cloth and a hot iron. Fold the corners over neatly to avoid any large bumps that will show on the other side.

2 Draw a deep border around all four sides using a pencil and ruler (keep the pencil line as faint as possible). My 122cm/48in cloth has a border of 20cm/8in. Spread lots of newspaper under the cloth prior to painting.

3 Paint in the central area first using two coats of a bright emulsion paint. Brush the paint up to the drawn line but don't despair too much if your line is a little wobbly, it all adds to the character of the cloth. Paint the border using two coats. Allow to dry thoroughly.

4 Enlarge the tulip outline on this page to a suitable size on a photocopier and transfer it on to a piece of manila paper. Cut around the outline carefully using a craft knife. (Thin cardboard will do if you first cut out the design and protect the cardboard with two layers of oil-based paint.)

5 Place small pieces of double-sided tape underneath the stencil and lay the stencil on the border. Stencil tulips using coloured emulsion or acrylic paints, angling one into each corner. Measure the distance between each corner stencil and space more tulips evenly between.

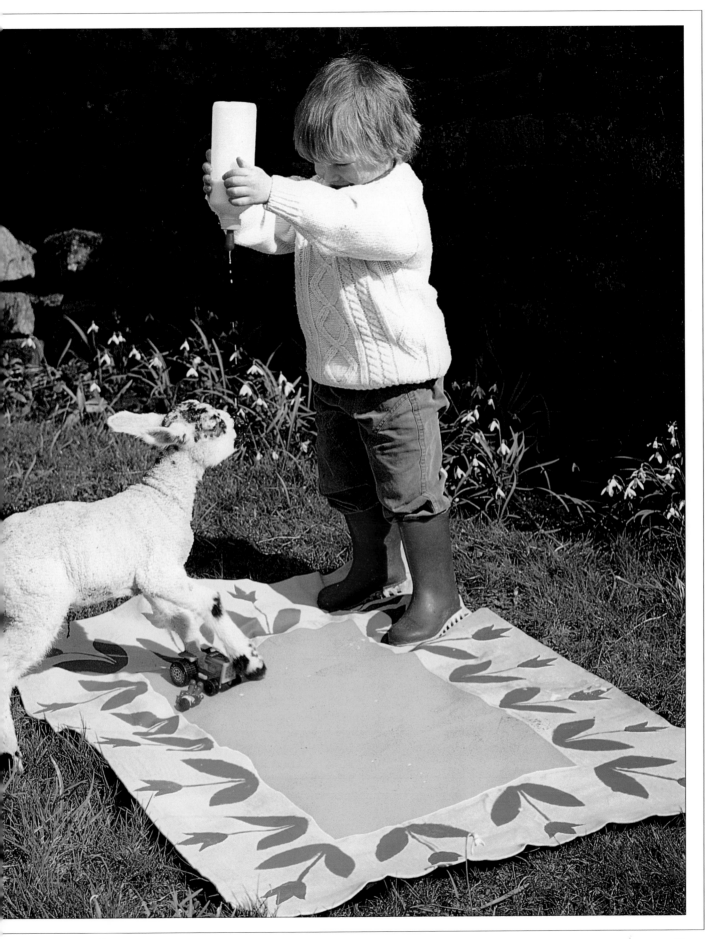

Scrolled Picture Frame

Although it's not edible, decorating this frame is just like icing a cake.

MATERIALS

coloured emulsion paint

filler

plastic container

mixing brush

thick paper

sticky tape

scissors

frame

Hints

There's no need to be confined to scrolls when decorating your picture frames: pipe the filler into zigzags or circles, even straight lines look just as good.

1 Mix equal quantities of paint and filler in the plastic container, adding a little more of either until you have made a thick paste; it will take a few minutes of stirring to get rid of any lumps. Twist a square of paper into a cone and secure it with sticky tape.

2 Drop the paint filler mixture into the cone with a teaspoon and roll the top down as you would an ordinary piping bag. Snip off the end of the cone and pipe the decoration on to the frame. Keep on piping the mixture until the frame is covered entirely, and leave it to dry before reassembling.

Hat Boxes

A tower of these boxes looks attractive as well as providing valuable storage space in a bedroom.

MATERIALS

hat boxes

coloured emulsion paints

paintbrush

copyright-free print borders

scissors

PVA adhesive

glue brush

saucer

cloth

Hints

Black-and-white copyright-free books provide a wealth of source material for lots of craft ideas, including this one.

1 Paint the hat boxes using toning emulsion paints - I used these pretty ice cream colours, but strong primaries would work just as well. Photocopy the page of border designs until you have enough of each design to wrap around a hatbox. Cut out each border.

2 Glue each border section around the edge of the hat boxes, using your fingers to smooth each section down to remove any small air bubbles. Butt the ends up to each other carefully as any overlaps will spoil the border.

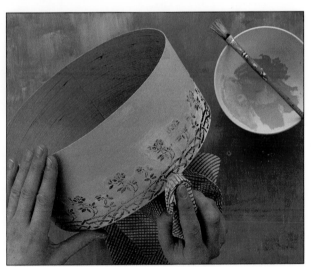

3 Mix together a little of the base colour emulsion paint with an equal quantity of water and brush this quickly over the paper border. Wipe a cloth over the surface of the paint before it has had a chance to dry, removing more paint from the printed areas and less from the cut edge. Leave to dry.

Painted Chair

Junk shops are great places for finding good quality, sturdy chairs such as this one, and with the minimum of preparation and a quick paint finish they are totally transformed.

MATERIALS

chair

sandpaper (medium grade)

wood mouldings

wood glue

glue brush

2 colours of emulsion paint

paintbrush

Hints

If you can find old chairs in junk shops, it would cost very little to have a complete set of chairs decorated in this way.

1 Prepare the surface of the chair for painting. If your chair is varnished as mine was, sandpaper is all you need to use for a smooth finish. Use wood glue to glue the mouldings in place. Leave the glue to dry thoroughly before starting to paint.

2 Paint the first emulsion layer on the chair and allow this to dry thoroughly before painting on the second colour. Distressing colour in this way is always more successful if the darkest paint is applied last.

3 Use the sandpaper to wear away some of the second colour to reveal the first colour underneath. If you accidentally remove too much paint so that you can see the wood itself, simply use a little of the top-colour emulsion to paint this in.

Chair Seat Cover

This chair has a drop-in seat
which is perfect for this
checkerboard cover made
from two colours of inexpensive
cotton fabric.

MATERIALS

seat base

2 colours of cotton fabric

scissors

sewing machine

thread

staple gun

Hints

Once made, protect the chair covers
with spray-on fabric guard which repels
everyday spills and splashes.

1 Cut the fabric into 7.5cm/3in-wide
strips. The strips must be long enough
to cover the seat base and turn to the
underside where they will be stapled. Make
two panels, each consisting of four strips
machine sewn together. Cut one panel into
7.5cm/3in pieces.

2 Sew three cut-off pieces of fabric
together along the narrow edges to
make a long strip and repeat. Sew the two
resulting strips together along their length to
form a checker pattern. Stitch this along the
edge of the central panel. Sew together
another checker panel and stitch this along
the other side.

3 Trim the fabric to fit the seat base,
press. Lay the seat base on the wrong
side of the fabric, pull the edges over on to
the wooden frame and staple in place. Staple
the centre of each edge and work outwards
to the corners. Fold the corners neatly and
drop the seat into the frame of the chair.

Seashell Cabinet

This cabinet can be hung on the wall or placed on a surface to be used as a glass-lidded display box for pretty soaps and bathroom accessories.

MATERIALS

bathroom cabinet

sandpaper (medium and fine grades)

thin cardboard

pencil

scissors

masking fluid

fine paintbrush

coloured emulsion paints

paintbrush

acrylic varnish

Hints

Paint starfish or fishes on this box as an alternative to these pink scallop shells.

1 Remove any old layers of paint or varnish if you are recycling an old cabinet. Transfer the shell on this page on to thin cardboard and cut along the outline carefully to make a simple stencil. Place the stencil on the cabinet and hold in place. Paint masking fluid between the shell outline and allow to dry.

2 Paint the base colour emulsion over the cabinet; for a more interesting effect, brush the colour on patchily. When the emulsion paint is quite dry, rub the surface of the masking fluid with your finger to start the peeling process, then peel it away to reveal the bare wood. Rub the surface lightly with sandpaper.

3 Paint the scallop shells using patchy areas of pink colour - don't worry if some of the raw wood shows through. When this is dry, add the fine shell details using a fine paintbrush. Seal and protect the cabinet with two layers of acrylic varnish.

Curtain Trimmings

Homemade trimmings are so simple to make you'll wonder why you never made them before.

MATERIALS

coloured canvas

sewing machine

thread

scissors

Hints

Use a contrasting thread for the best effect. If you can't find a colour of canvas to suit your requirements, you could dye natural canvas in a washing machine.

1 Cut long 7.5cm/3in-wide strips of canvas. Fray the edges by teasing the threads open in the weave, then pull them down through the length of the fabric. Fray each strip to a depth of 2.5cm/1in.

2 Set your sewing machine to an embroidery stitch, if it has one, or a close zigzag if it doesn't. Use contrasting thread. Sew two lines of stitches along the length of each strip, keeping the lines as close to each other as you can.

3 Sew the strips together to make lengths as long as you require. Press the seams open and trim the raw edge along the length. Turn this edge under, then stitch the trimming on to your furnishings, keeping the stitching line as close to the folded edge as possible.

Curtain Banner

Tight budgets needn't mean scrimping on beautiful fabrics.
This curtain uses two half-widths of fabric and yet still gives the
impression of a full curtain.

MATERIALS

patterned fabric	trimming fabric for ties
iron and ironing board	string
sewing machine	needle
thread	muslin
scissors	fabric dye

Hints

Measure the curtain drop, add 5cm/2in for seam allowances and the allowance required for
pattern matching, then halve the measurement - giving you the length for your patterned fabric.

1 Cut the selvages from the edges of the
fabric and fold the fabric in half down
the length. Press, then cut the fabric into two
halves. Sew the two halves of fabric together
across the width, matching the pattern if
necessary. Press this seam open.

2 Turn over the upper and lower hems
and sew the trimming down the sides
of the fabric, keeping the line of stitching
close to the edge of the fabric. Make sure
the raw fabric edge is not visible behind the
fringe when viewed from the front.

3 To make the curtain ring ties, cut strips
measuring 7.5 x 38cm/3 x 15in from the
fabric. Fold them in half enclosing a piece of
string in one end. Sew across the width,
trapping the string in the stitches, and then
down the length. Pull the end of the string
to draw the tie through to the right side, and
sew the end closed.

4 Calculate the amount of muslin you
need to cover the window: allow one
and-a-half times the width of the frame plus
5cm/2in hem all round. Dye the muslin, dry,
then press. Stitch the hems and sew the
panel centrally on the muslin. Stitch the ties
across the width of the curtain and tie to the
curtain pole.

Sink Cabinet

This cabinet has a real beachcomber look, even the handles are made from pieces of driftwood.

MATERIALS

cabinet

white acrylic primer

2 colours of emulsion paint

paintbrush

sandpaper (coarse and medium grades)

Hints

Choose colours that are close in tone for this cabinet and wear the colours away as little or as much as you like - continually assess the distressing process as you work.

1 Paint the cabinet with the white acrylic primer and allow to dry. Make sure all the wood is covered well as the humid conditions in a bathroom are not very kind to wooden furniture.

2 Loosely brush on coats of coloured emulsion paint, layering one coat on top of another but allowing one coat to dry before applying the next. Don't worry about trying to achieve an even layer of colour.

3 Sand the whole cabinet down using first coarse then medium grade sandpaper, controlling the amount of paint removal as you work.

4 Screw a handle in place, or use a piece of driftwood if you prefer.

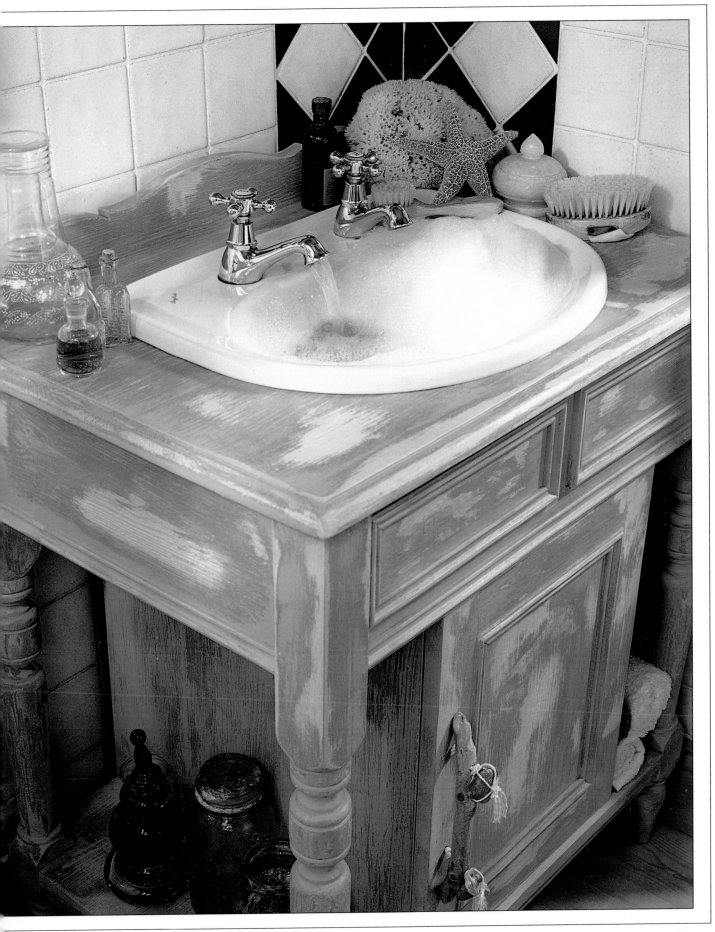

Mirror Frame

Cut your own frame from a piece of plywood using a small fret saw.

MATERIALS

frame

coloured emulsion paint

paintbrush

mirror tile

self-adhesive pads

aluminium cans

tin snips

nail

enamel paint

fine paintbrush

hammer

piece of wood

tacks

picture fasteners

Hints

Use gloves to protect your hands as you cut open the cans because they can be very sharp. Cut your frame into any shape you like - my crown is quite dramatic, you may prefer a heart or diamond, or a regular square. The only consideration is that the mirror tile should fit inside the shape with a narrow border around the sides.

1 Paint the frame and stick the mirror tile in place with the self-adhesive pads aligning it centrally within the frame. Cut the tops and bottoms from the cans and cut a seam down the middle to flatten each one. Trim away any sharp edges.

2 Lay the flattened sheets over the frame and cut the metal into shaped pieces that will fit within the edges of the frame. You may need to use different sections of metal to cover the frame, these should overlap if possible. If you have an unusual shape, like this crown, mark the metal before cutting.

3 When each piece of metal is cut, use the nail to scratch in star and coil shapes on the wrong side. Press hard so that the outlines show through on the right side. Paint the different sections with the enamel paint and allow to dry.

4 Punch a line of decorative holes along the outside edges of each metal section using the nail and hammer. You will find it quicker and easier to punch along a piece of wood - any small piece of scrap wood will do.

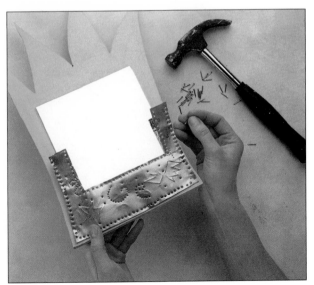

5 Attach the metal pieces to the frame with small tacks. Use several tacks around the corners and angles to make sure that these edges do not lift up and scratch. Attach picture fasteners to the back of the frame to hang it on a wall.

Star Lampshade

When the light is switched on, the stars illuminate the delicate tissue paper.

MATERIALS

thin paper

pencil

lampshade

craft knife

2 colours of emulsion or water-based paint

paintbrush

tissue paper

paper/fabric adhesive

glue brush

Hints

If you have acrylic or gouache water-based colours, use these rather than the emulsion colours. However, you will need to apply the base colour thickly to achieve an opaque finish. The second colour needs to be diluted to splatter successfully.

1 Lay the thin paper over the star motifs on this page and draw around their edges using a pencil. Press the paper to the inside of the lampshade until you can see the outlines of the stars showing through. Draw these star shapes randomly over the lampshade.

2 Cut around the drawn pencil outlines on the shade using a sharp craft knife. Always work with the blade away from you and cut through the fabric shade slowly and carefully. Paint the shade using the base colour. Allow to dry, then splatter the thinner, second colour over the first to create a speckled finish.

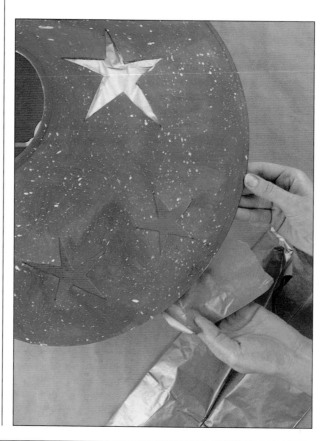

3 For each of the stars, tear a piece of tissue paper slightly larger than the outlines and glue to the inside of the frame using adhesive. Before the adhesive is dry, use the craft knife to cut the excess tissue paper at the back of the shade into star shapes. When the light is switched on, these outlines will be visible through the shade.

Bedroom Wall Treatment

A simple motif such as this one is easy to cut if you follow these steps. If your stencil is to follow a regular pattern, measure out and mark a grid of squares on the walls using a tape measure and place the stencil in the centre of each square. Alternatively, place the stencil on the walls at random.

MATERIALS

pencil

manila paper

craft knife

double-sided tape

gold acrylic paint

stencil brush

Hints

If you cannot find manila paper, use thin cardboard. First cut your stencil, then paint the cardboard with two layers of oil-based paint and leave to dry before stencilling. The paint prevents the cardboard from becoming soggy.

1 Use a photocopier to enlarge the size of the motif on this page and transfer the image on to the manila paper. Cut around the outline using a sharp craft knife.

2 Hold the stencil in place with double-sided tape. Dip the stencil brush into the paint, dab off the excess and then apply the paint using a stippling motion with the brush. Peel off the stencil and repeat.

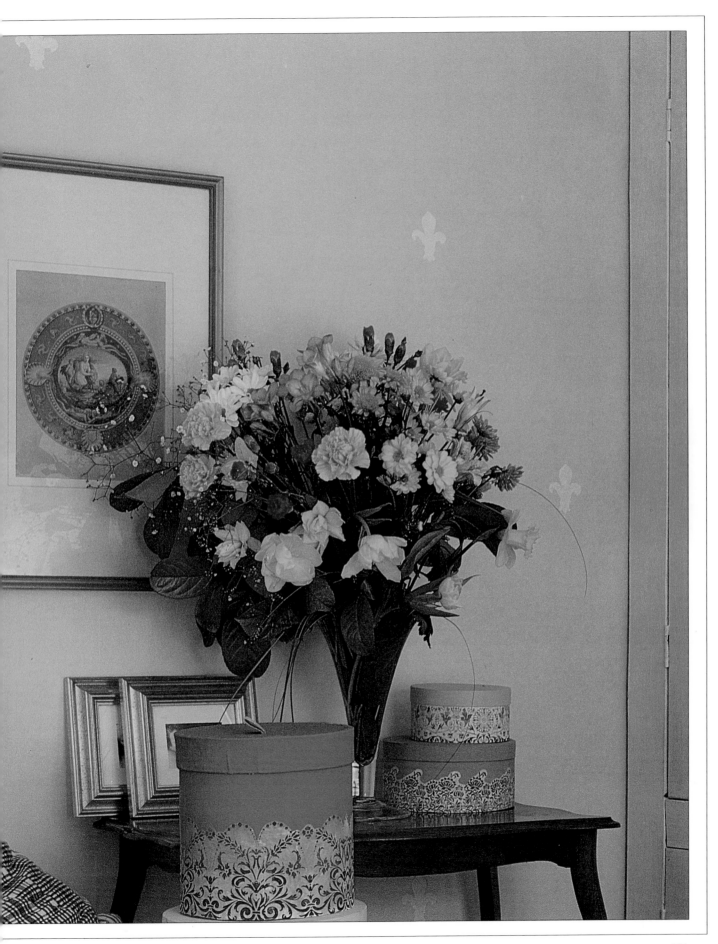

ACKNOWLEDGMENTS

The publishers would like to thank the following companies for providing the merchandise used in our photographs.

Accessories The Pier, 200 Tottenham Court Road, London W1P 0AD
The General Trading Company, 144 Sloane Street, Sloane Square, London SW1

Paints Dulux ICI Paints, Wexham Road, Slough, Berks (Customer Advice Tel: 0753 550555)

Woodcraft Products Somerset Creative Products, Charlecot, Mark Causeway, Mark, Somerset TA9 4PX

GLOSSARY

US readers may not be familiar with the following terms:

UK	US
aluminium	aluminum
Bondaweb	fusible webbing
biscuit tin	cookie tin
car boot sale	yard or garage sale
chinagraph pencil	chinagraph marker
curtain rail	curtain rod or track
emulsion paint	latex paint
fret saw	scroll saw
hardboard	masonite
hessian	burlap
junk shop	secondhand store or thrift shop
lining paper	plain shelf paper
matt	matte or flat finish
mount (for pictures)	mat
muslin	cheesecloth
notice board	bulletin board
noughts and crosses	tic-tac-toe
panel pins	brads
PVA adhesive	white or yellow craft glue
roller blind	window shade
rubbish	trash, garbage
wadding	batting
zip	zipper